8/10

11-2/2012-6/12
13-2/2014-12/14
14-1/2015-12/15

The Apache

Liz Sonneborn

Watts LIBRARY™

Franklin Watts
A Division of Scholastic Inc.
New York • Toronto • London • Auckland • Sydney
Mexico City • New Delhi • Hong Kong
Danbury, Connecticut

Note to readers: Definitions for words in **bold** can be found in the Glossary at the back of this book.

Photographs © 2005: Allan Houser Foundation/Bela Kalman, Boston: 47; Corbis Images: 16, 31 (Bettmann), 20 (David Muench), 4 (NASA), 48, 49 (Tony Roberts), 3 top, 18, 29, 33, 36; Getty Images/John N. Choate/MPI: 39; Hulton|Archive/Getty Images: 35; Library of Congress: 22, 40, 43; Mary Evans Picture Library: 14; Nativestock.com/Marilynn "Angel" Wynn: 8, 10, 32, 50; Network Aspen/David Hiser: 3 bottom, 11, 44, 45, 51; North Wind Picture Archives: 12; Peter Arnold Inc./Bernd Jonkmanns/Bilderberg: 6; Photri Inc.: 28; Superstock, Inc.: 26; Time Life Pictures/Getty Images/National Archives: 24.

Cover illustration by Gary Overacre

Map by XNR Productions Inc.

Library of Congress Cataloging-in-Publication Data

Sonneborn, Liz.
   The Apache / Liz Sonneborn
      p. cm. — (Watts library)
   Includes bibliographical references and index.
   ISBN 0-531-12295-6 (lib. bdg.)   0-531-16717-8 (pbk.)
   1. Apache Indians—History.   2. Apache Indians—Social life and customs. I. Title. II. Series.
E99.A6S64 2005
979.004'9725—dc22

2004014315

Contents

Chapter One

Beginnings

Long ago, the world was terrorized by four monsters. White-Painted Woman prayed for help. A spirit named Life Giver came to her. He told White-Painted Woman that she would have a baby. This baby, named Child of the Water, would save her from the monsters.

While still a boy, Child of the Water said he was ready to fight. His mother gave him a bow and arrow made of wood. The first monster Child of the Water encountered was Owl-Man Giant. He challenged the boy to a contest, during which each would shoot four arrows at

Fort Apache reservation in Arizona is one of the many places members of Apache tribes live today.

the other. Owl-Man Giant went first. All of his arrows missed Child of the Water. Then it was Child of the Water's turn. His first three arrows also missed their mark. But the fourth struck Owl-Man Giant's heart.

Child of the Water then killed Buffalo Monster, Eagle Monster, and Antelope Monster. With the monsters gone, the world was finally safe for the first human beings.

Becoming Apache

This is just one version of the story of Child of the Water, which has long been told by the Apache Indians. Their ancestors once lived in what is now northwestern Canada. Over time, they traveled south. By about 1400, they arrived in the American Southwest.

One group of these Indians became the Navajo **tribe**. The

rest became known as the Apache. They eventually divided into six tribes called the Chiricahua, Jicarilla, Mescalero, Western, Lipan, and Plains Apache. These Apache tribes claimed territory in what is now northern Mexico, Arizona, New Mexico, Colorado, Oklahoma, and Texas.

The Apache tribes had similar languages and customs. But the Apache did not act as one people, ruled by a single leader. Scattered over a large territory, they lived in small groups made up of several families. The Apache generally felt a stronger bond to these small groups than to their tribes.

The Apache Way

Among the Apache, family members usually lived close to one another. A couple and their children had their own home. But nearby were the houses of their grandparents, uncles, aunts, and cousins. All of them worked together to obtain food and other necessities.

When a couple married, the husband came to live with his wife's family. He was expected to work hard to help support her relatives. If he was lazy or treated his wife badly, they would drive him out of their camp.

Most Apache lived in **wickiups**, which are dome-shaped houses made from wooden sticks covered with grass, brush, or animal hides. Some Apache made **tipis**. These portable cone-shaped dwellings were also used by Plains tribes living to the east of their lands.

The Apache lived in a harsh environment. It was often

The Apache's traditional homes are called wickiups and made from wood and brush or animal hides.

difficult to get enough food to eat. Families had to move their camps several times a year. Each season, they traveled to areas with the most comfortable climate and the greatest number of wild animals and plants.

Apache men hunted antelope, deer, and rabbits. Like their other Plains Indian neighbors, some Lipan and Plains Apache hunters also stalked buffalo. Apache women gathered many wild foods, including berries, nuts, and roots.

Some Apache living in the western portion of their territory were farmers. They learned farming techniques from the Pueblo Indians, who had lived in the Southwest for hundreds of years. These Apache grew corn, beans, and squash, but these foods made up just a small part of their diet.

Working Women

In Apache society, women were well-respected for their hard work. Every day, they gathered food, cooked meals, and hauled wood for the household fire. They also wove beautiful baskets to carry food or even their children. Most Apache women spent their lives caring for their families. But some became leaders, healers, and warriors. Perhaps the most famous Apache female warrior was Lozen, who fought against U.S. soldiers alongside the famous leader Geronimo during the nineteenth century.

Warring and Raiding

The decision of when and where to move was made by a local leader. This leader was a man who had earned the respect of all the other people in his group. He never ordered his followers to do anything. Instead, he persuaded them that his plan was best. If he lost the confidence of his followers, they quickly replaced him with a new leader.

Leaders also helped organize war parties. During wartime, groups sometimes came together to form a band, made up of several hundred people. Bands were most commonly found among the Western Apache and the Chiricahua Apache.

Most often, the Apache fought wars to take revenge. If a person was murdered by enemy Indians, his relatives called for a war to punish the killers. Boys were trained for war at an early age. They raced, wrestled, and fought play battles.

Apache warriors also staged raids. During a raid, men and boys sneaked up on the village of an enemy. Quietly, they stole food, weapons, supplies, and animals. Sometimes, the warriors were able to make off with these goods without even encountering the enemy. Since food was scarce in Apache territory, raiding often kept the Apache from going hungry.

Harnessing Power

The Apache also ensured their well-being by performing ceremonies. A successful war, for instance, was celebrated with a ceremonial dance, during which the dancers acted out feats of bravery. Ceremonies were also held to cure the sick and to mark important moments in peoples' lives. They were often overseen by **shamans**. These religious leaders were usually men, but particularly powerful women could also become shamans.

Skilled shamans were able to control the supernatural power the Apache saw in all things. This power could be used for good. It could hurt enemies, protect people from attack, and destroy disease. But it could also be used for evil. The Apache greatly feared witches, who had the power to make people ill. People who acted strangely were often accused of practicing witchcraft. Anyone proven guilty was burned to death.

The Apache also feared the dead. According to their religious beliefs, when people died, their ghosts traveled to the afterlife. But some ghosts became lonely there and returned to the world. Often, they appeared in the shape of an owl or a coyote. Just the sight of a ghost could make someone sick. Fainting, insanity, and bad dreams were just a few signs of ghost sickness.

To guide ghosts to the afterworld and keep them there, the Apache carefully performed funeral ceremonies. When a person died, his relatives wept, cut their hair, and put on old clothing. The body was washed, dressed, and buried with the dead's personal possessions.

Afterward, no one ever said the dead person's name out loud. His relatives

An Apache shaman holds a medicine skin.

The Sunrise Dance

One of the most important Apache ceremonies was the Nai-hes, also known as Na ii ees or the Sunrise Dance. It was performed to mark a girl's passage into womanhood.

A girl's relatives spent months preparing for her Sunrise Dance. They selected a sacred area for the ceremony, chose a holy man to perform it, and planned a great feast. The girl's mother and grandmother also sewed her a ceremonial dress. It would give the girl the power of White-Painted Woman, the mythic heroine who helped create the Apache world.

For four days and nights, those attending the ceremony feasted, danced, gambled, and visited with one another. The girl was instructed about how to live a good and proper life. She also helped anyone who was feeling sick, since White-Painted Woman's power allowed her heal the ill. At the end of the Sunrise Dance, the girl plunged a stick into the ground to tell everyone that she had become an Apache woman.

might even move their camp, so his ghost would not be able to find them if it decided to come back to Earth. By following these rituals, the Apache made the world healthy for the living.

The arrival of the Spanish in the 1500s changed the lives of the Apache forever.

Chapter Two

Outsiders

In the Southwest, the Apache had contact with many different Indian tribes. Some were their friends. Others were their enemies. But in the sixteenth century, they met a new people different from any other they had encountered before. These people were Spaniards who traveled from Europe to find riches in North America.

The first Spaniards to arrive were soldiers looking for gold. Soon they were followed by men, women, and children sent by the Spanish government to settle there. By the time the Spanish began venturing into Apache territory, they had already established settlements to the south in present-day Mexico.

Dealing with the Spanish

At first, the Apache had little direct contact with the Spanish. Since the Apache traveled from place to place over a large territory, they rarely came upon these strangers. The Pueblo Indians, their neighbors to the west, were not so lucky. They lived in permanent villages that were often attacked by the Spanish. The Spanish had a huge advantage in these battles. They had European guns, while the Pueblo fought with bows and arrows. With their superior weapons, the Spanish were able to defeat the Pueblo and take over their villages.

The Spanish sold many Apache into slavery. Some Apache slaves were forced to work in mines in Mexico.

To escape Spanish rule, some Pueblo Indians fled. A few came to live among the Apache. They probably introduced the Apache to horses, which the Spanish had brought to North America. The Apache quickly learned to ride these animals. On horseback, they could travel farther distances than ever before, allowing them to make new trading partners. The Apache also liked horses for their tasty meat.

By the late 1500s, Spanish settlers were moving into Apache territory. It became harder for the Apache to avoid the Spanish. Increasingly, the two groups warred with each other. Often, the Spanish attacked the Apache just so they could take captives. Apache captives were often sent to the Spanish capital of Mexico City and sold as slaves.

Raiding the Enemy

In one way, however, the Apache actually welcomed the arrival of Spanish settlers. Spanish settlements were stocked with all kinds of goods. By raiding the Spanish, the Apache had a steady supply of food, horses, and guns. Apache raiding parties became bigger and bigger. Eventually, the Apache became dependent on raiding Spanish settlements for the necessities of life.

The constant raiding took a toll on the Spanish. They not only lost huge amounts of supplies. They also lost many men in their constant battles against Apache raiders. The Spanish built forts along their northern border and sent more and more soldiers to protect them. But by the mid-1700s, they seemed to be losing their war with the Apache. The Indians had killed thousands of soldiers and stolen millions of dollars of property. The Spanish began to wonder if maintaining their northern settlements was worth all this trouble.

In 1786, Spanish leader Bernardo de Gálvez came up with a new plan for dealing with the Apache. The Spanish began trying to negotiate peace with willing Apache groups. The Spanish encouraged these Apache to move to villages near their forts.

Bernardo de Gálvez wanted to make peace with the Apache.

There, the Spanish gave the Apache food, cloth, and other supplies. The gifts were not just tokens of friendships. They were also intended to make the Apache dependent. If the Apache came to rely on these gifts, they might stop attacking the Spanish once and for all.

Meeting Mexicans

The Spanish and Apache continued to fight from time to time. But, for the most part, Gálvez's plan worked until the beginning of the 1800s. Then, Spanish officials faced a problem even larger than the Apache. Starting in 1810, many poor Spaniards rose up against their rulers. After a long and bloody rebellion, they won their freedom from Spain in 1821. The Spanish lands in North America then became the independent country of Mexico.

The Apache were hardly aware of these political changes. But they certainly noticed that they were receiving fewer and fewer gifts. Mexico had many debts after its war for independence. Its government could not afford to give away the goods the Apache expected. Annoyed, the Apache began attacking Mexican settlements, and Mexico sent soldiers north to fight them.

The Apache came to dislike the Mexicans as much as they had the Spanish. But soon they would meet an even more dangerous enemy—American soldiers and settlers determined to take over Apache lands.

War with the Comanche

By the late seventeenth century, the Jicarilla Apache's lands were still threatened by a particularly fierce foe, the Comanche Indians. Armed with guns they obtained from their French allies, the Comanche fought the Jicarilla on and off for decades. The wars came to an end in the 1780s, when the Spanish, aided by Jicarilla warriors, finally repelled the Comanche's advance.

of a competent tribunal, shall be punished by the confiscation of the property so attempted to be fraudulently introduced.

Article XIX.

With respect to all merchandise, effects and property whatsoever, imported into ports of Mexico whilst in the occupation of the forces of the United States, whether by citizens of either republic, or by citizens or subjects of any neutral nation, the following rules shall be observed:

I. All such merchandise, effects and property, if imported previously to the restoration of the Custom Houses to the Mexican Authorities, as stipulated for in the third Article of this treaty, shall be exempt from confiscation, although the importation of the same be prohibited by the Mexican tariff.

Artículo XIX.

Respecto de los efectos, mercancías y propiedades importados en los puertos mexicanos durante el tiempo que han estado ocupados por las fuerzas de los Estados Unidos, sea por ciudadanos de cualquiera de las dos Repúblicas, sea por ciudadanos ó subditos de alguna nacion neutral, se observarán las reglas siguientes.

I. Los dichos efectos, mercancías y propiedades siempre que se hayan importado antes de la restitucion de las Aduanas á las autoridades mexicanas con forme ... ticulo ... guardarán libres de la pena de =

The United States received most of the Apache homeland from Mexico when both countries signed the Treaty of Guadalupe Hidalgo.

Chapter Three

Under American Rule

In 1846, war broke out between Mexico and the United States. After less than two years of fighting, Mexico was defeated. In exchange for peace, it gave the United States about half its territory. This territory included most of the Apache homeland.

At first, the Apache were friendly to Americans. Some Apache even joined their side during the war. But quickly, the Indians came to distrust the Americans moving into their territory. Some were just traveling through Apache lands on the way to California, where gold had been discovered. But others were settling down, building homes and farms on Apache hunting grounds.

Broken Promises

To the Apache, the settlers were unwelcome intruders. But to the settlers, the Apache were in the way. In settlers' eyes, Apache territory now belonged to the United States. They thought the Apache should move aside, as they took control of the tribes' best land.

Many Apache, however, were not willing to give up their territory without a fight. They raided American settlements just as they had Mexican settlements. To protect the settlers, the U.S. Army sent soldiers to battle the Apache. During the

Fort Bowie in Arizona is one of the forts built by U.S. Army to protect settlers from Apache raids.

1850s, they built forts throughout what are now New Mexico and Arizona. Still, the American forces had little success in ending Apache raids.

Some American officials tried dealing with the Apache in a different way. They made **treaties** with various Apache groups. In these agreements, both sides promised not to fight with one another. But these treaties, often broken by the U.S. government, did little to end the violence. In 1851, for instance, the Jicarilla Apache in what is now New Mexico signed a treaty with the U.S. government, which pledged to give them food and other supplies. But when the government failed to provide these goods, the Jicarilla resumed their raiding.

The Chiricahua at War

The Chiricahua Apache's experiences with Americans were even more bitter. In the early 1850s, gold was discovered in Chiricahua territory in what is now southwestern New Mexico. American miners flooded into the area. Their presence worried the Chiricahua, especially Mangas Coloradas. Tall, intelligent, and courageous, Mangas was a very well-respected leader. He met with the miners and suggested that they leave Apache territory. The Americans responded by tying him up and beating him almost to death.

The Chiricahua considered the attack on Mangas a vicious insult. They turned against all Americans, attacking settlements and wagons carrying mail. The fighting continued for years. Finally, a U.S. official named Michael Steck tried to

The attack on Mangas, an important leader, greatly upset the Chiricahua.

make peace. He met with Cochise, a Chiricahua leader who was also Mangas's son-in-law, at Apache Pass in what is now southeastern Arizona. Cochise agreed to end the attacks.

Well known for his honesty, Cochise kept his word until 1860. At that time, a group of about fifty soldiers led by Lieutenant George Bascom rode into Chiricahua territory looking for Cochise. Bascom was convinced Cochise had led a raid on a nearby ranch, during which a twelve-year-old boy was taken captive.

Cochise, with a few warriors, arrived at Apache Pass to meet with Bascom. The Apache carried a white flag, a signal they came in peace. After greeting the Americans, Cochise and his men entered Bascom's tent. Once inside, Bascom immediately accused Cochise of raiding the ranch and taking the boy. When Cochise denied he was involved, Bascom called him a liar. Fearing for his life, Cochise pulled out a knife, sliced the tent, slipped through the opening, and ran to safety as the Americans opened fire.

It was later proved that Cochise and his warriors had

had nothing to do with the raid. Even so, the warriors that remained in the camp were executed by Bascom's troops. The "Cut the Tent" incident angered Cochise. He was once willing to talk friendship with Americans. Now all he wanted was war.

Bosque Redondo

As the conflict with the Chiricahua heated up, the United States faced another war. States in the South wanted to break away and start their own country. The states in the North decided to fight to stop them. The result was the American Civil War, which lasted from 1861 to 1865.

At first, the Civil War was good news for the Apache. Many U.S. soldiers left Apache territory to go fight for the North. But in early 1862, a group of volunteer soldiers from California rode into Apache territory. Led by General James H. Carleton, they were officially charged with maintaining order in New Mexico Territory (now Arizona and New Mexico). Unofficially, they were looking for gold and other precious minerals.

Life at Bosque Redondo reservation was very difficult for the Mescalero.

To gain control of mineral-rich lands, Carleton decided to round up southwestern Indians and confine them on a **reservation**. Carleton led a series of attacks on the Chiricahua but could not conquer them. He had more success with a bloody campaign against the Navajo and the Mescalero Apache. After killing hundreds, Carleton's troops led nine thousand Navajo and five hundred Mescalero to the Bosque Redondo reservation.

Life at Bosque Redondo was a nightmare for the Mescalero. Crammed with the Navajo on the tiny reservation, they barely had enough food and water to survive. To save themselves, most of the Mescalero escaped and fled into the mountains.

The Camp Grant Massacre

The Western Apache learned from the experiences of the Chiricahua and Mescalero. They generally tried to avoid conflict with Americans. Despite their efforts, however, they suffered a horrible tragedy at the hands of angry settlers.

Early in 1871, about 150 Western Apache appeared at Camp Grant, an army post in present-day Arizona. The Indians used to live in the area, but, fearing violence, they had fled into the mountains. Tired and hungry, the Western Apache wanted to return home. They approached the officers at Camp Grant, asking for permission to live nearby. The officers agreed and gave them some food **rations**. Soon, hundreds more Western Apache gathered at Camp Grant, seeking food and protection.

The people of the nearby town of Tucson were upset when they heard what was happening at Camp Grant. Victims of Apache raids, the townspeople hated the Apache and wanted to drive them out of the region. Accompanied by a group of Papago Indians, longtime enemies of the Apache, a mob from Tucson entered Camp Grant. They murdered about one hundred Western Apache as they slept. With many of the men away on a hunting expedition, most of the victims were women and children.

The people of Tucson celebrated when they learned of the Camp Grant **Massacre**. They thought the Apache got what they deserved. But many Americans were disgusted by the news. Among them was President Ulysses S. Grant. The mob called the attack justice, but he declared it was "purely murder."

President Ulysses S. Grant thought that peace could be achieved with the Apache. He wanted to move all of the western Indians to reservations.

Chapter Four

The Apache Wars

Even before the Camp Grant Massacre, President Grant began rethinking the treatment of the Apache by the United States. Warring with them, he decided, was not working. Grant came up with a new plan named the Peace Policy. It was designed to end all fighting between Indians and settlers.

The Peace Policy called for all western Indians to be sent to reservations. There, American soldiers would protect the Indians from attack by angry settlers.

On reservations, the Indians would also be taught to farm. Once they grew enough food to feed themselves, Grant thought, Indians would have no reason to raid American settlements.

The Peace Policy

In the 1870s, the U.S. government established several Apache reservations in present-day Arizona and New Mexico. American officials told all Apache Indians to report to these areas. Any Apache who did not go to a reservation willingly would be hunted down by the U.S. Army.

Some Apache were tired of war. They went to the reservations without a fight. But many were disappointed by what

Tired of fighting, many of the Apache reached an agreement with U.S. officials to move to the reservations.

Moving to the reservations did little to help the Apache with their problems with the settlers.

they found there. The Apache's best territory had already been taken over by non-Indians. The reservations were usually located on land no one wanted.

The United States also did little to protect the reservation Apache. For instance, in 1873, it gave the Mescalero a reservation along the Tularosa River in what is now New Mexico. But American officials did nothing to stop settlers from overrunning the reservation and stealing the Mescalero's livestock. Instead of guarding the Indians and their property, U.S. soldiers bullied the Mescalero, killing dozens of Apache men.

Cochise and Jeffords

In 1867, the Chiricahua had just killed fourteen employees of Thomas J. Jeffords, a stagecoach driver and former army scout. Jeffords decided he had to confront Cochise about the matter. Alone, the two men discussed the situation. During the meeting, they not only established an informal peace. They also began a close friendship.

In 1872, when the army was pursuing Cochise, General O. O. Howard asked Jeffords to help him talk with Cochise. Howard knew Jeffords was the only white man Cochise completely trusted. Together, the three men hashed out a plan to establish a reservation just for the Chiricahua. With Cochise's support, Jeffords was hired to be the reservation's **agent**. As agent, Jeffords was an official of the U.S. government. Still, he always tried to do what was best for Cochise's people.

Two years after Jeffords's appointment, Cochise died. Jeffords knew where Cochise was buried but kept the location to himself. He feared non-Indian vandals might destroy the grave. He knew that, among whites, Cochise had many enemies, but just one true and loyal friend.

The Chiricahua Resist

Understandably, some Apache did not want to live on reservations. The Chiricahua were especially resistant. Among those distrustful of the Peace Policy was Cochise. He and his followers at first agreed to move to a reservation. But when the U.S. government refused to set aside land for them in their old territory, they fled.

General O. O. Howard pursued the runaway Chiricahua. Howard followed them to the Dragoon Mountains. Bravely heading into the Chiricahua's hideout with only two other men, Howard met with Cochise. They made a deal. Cochise promised to take his people to a reservation, as long it was located in the Chiricahua's original homeland.

True to his word, Cochise led his followers to the new Chiricahua reservation. As they settled in, more Chiricahua flocked there. Even though tensions often rose between them and their non-Indian neighbors, Cochise worked hard to keep the peace until his death in 1874.

Escape from San Carlos

Soon after Cochise's death, the Chiricahua were dealt another blow. They learned that the U.S. government wanted to move them to San Carlos, another Apache reservation far from their home. Despite its promises to Cochise, the United States decided to shut down the Chiricahua reservation to save money.

By 1876, hundreds of Chiricahua had arrived at San Carlos. They hated it from the start. The land was dry, and air was hot and humid. One Chiricahua complained that the barren landscape was full of "stones and ashes and thorns, with some scorpions and rattlesnakes thrown in."

After initially objecting to moving to the reservations, Cochise agreed to take his people to a reservation in their original homeland.

The Chiricahua were moved to another reservation after Cochise's death. They had difficulty adjusting to the hostile desert environment of the San Carlos reservation.

Even worse, the Chiricahua had to share San Carlos with other Apache groups. They did not always get along. U.S. officials made the situation worse. They encouraged each group to spy on the others and report any bad behavior. Soon the Apache began to distrust each other as much as the Americans.

Six months after arriving in San Carlos, a Chiricahua leader named Victorio had had enough. He led three hundred Chiricahua out of the reservation. Most surrendered to the U.S. Army a few weeks later. But Victorio and a few devoted followers remained on the run. Fearing more Apache raids, non-Indian settlers in the area were sent into a panic.

The army chased after Victorio, driving his people south into Mexico. There, their flight ended in October 1880. Victorio died during a bloody battle with Mexican soldiers.

Geronimo's Fight

Victorio's defeat did little to quiet the Chiricahua's fighting spirit. Throughout the early 1880s, small groups of Chiricahua kept running away from San Carlos, with U.S. troops in pursuit. Among the most persistent of the Chiricahua rebels was Geronimo.

After fleeing and surrendering several times, Geronimo and about 130 followers escaped San Carlos in 1881. Led by General George Crook, the U.S. Army set out after them.

Geronimo (right) and some of his followers left the reservation only to be pursued by the U.S. Army.

With the soldiers were several Apache, who worked for the army as **scouts**.

Largely because of the scouts' help, Crook found Geronimo's hideout. Geronimo surrendered and promised to lead his followers back to San Carlos. But along the way, Geronomo changed his mind. With a few dozen men, he bolted for Mexico.

The army criticized Crook for allowing Geronimo to get away. It replaced him with General Nelson A. Miles. Miles would stop at nothing to catch Geronimo and his people.

With Mexico's permission, he led an army of five thousand soldiers across the border. As they closed in, the Chiricahua were running out of supplies and ammunition. On September 4, 1886, Geronimo surrendered for the last time. The Apache's wars with the U.S. Army were finally over.

Fort Marion

The runaway Chiricahua were not sent back to San Carlos. Nearby American settlers were terrified of Geronimo. They wanted him and all of the Chiricahua out of the Southwest for good.

The army gathered up about five hundred Chiricahua. Although some had served as scouts for the army, they were all branded as enemies of the United States. The Chiricahua were loaded on eastbound trains, which took them to Fort Marion, a prison in Florida.

Life at Fort Marion was terrible. Hundreds of prisoners were crowded into a small space. Some became ill, and disease spread quickly. One-fourth of the imprisoned Chiricahua died.

Many non-Indians, including General Crook, spoke out against the government's treatment of the Chiricahua. Under pressure, the United States eventually sent the Chiricahua to Fort Sill in present-day Oklahoma. There, in 1909, the mighty Geronimo died, far from his treasured homeland.

Many Apache imprisoned at Fort Marion in Florida became ill and some died.

35

Living on reservations proved difficult for the Apache. An Apache family is shown here outside of their wickiup made from canvas and wood scraps instead of traditional materials.

Chapter Five

Life on the Reservation

With Geronimo's surrender, the Apache ended their resistance to confinement on reservations. Years of battling the U.S. Army had left the Apache worn and exhausted. But they found little relief in their new homes. In fact, for many Apache, reservation life proved almost as difficult and dangerous as the Apache Wars had been.

Hunger and Disease

One of the biggest challenges for reservation Apache was dealing with Indian agents. An agent was an employee of the U.S. government charged with managing a reservation. Many agents assigned to the Apache were cruel and dishonest.

Some cheated the Apache out of food and supplies that the U.S. government had promised to give them. Others withheld food rations from anyone who did not do whatever they said. As a result, many Apache went hungry.

Weakened by lack of food, reservation residents often became sick. Diseases such as flu and pneumonia killed many people. Tuberculosis was also a problem. In 1917, the agent on the Jicarilla's reservation reported that nine out of ten children suffered from this serious lung disease.

New Ways

On reservations, the Apache way of life was also threatened. Agents were supposed to teach the Apache about non-Indian customs. At the same time, they tried to force the Apache to abandoned their old ways.

As part of this plan, Apache children were sent to government-run schools. There, they were taught to speak English, wear non-Indian clothes, and look down on Apache customs. To make students do as they were told, teachers sometimes took away their food or beat them.

Against their parents' wishes, some Apache children were

sent to boarding schools where they lived year-round. Their relatives were not allowed to visit them. Mistreated and scared, many students ran away.

Agents also encouraged **missionaries** to come to Apache reservations. Missionaries taught the Indians about the Christian religion. Some converted to Christianity. But many

Some Apache children were sent away to boarding schools far from their families.

39

The U.S. government tried to change the Apache's way of life and make them farmers instead of hunters.

Apache preferred their own religion. Defying the agents, they continued to perform traditional Apache ceremonies.

Another job of agents was to turn the Apache into farmers. Farming was the way most non-Indians made their living. If the Apache took up farming, the agents believed they might adopt other non-Indian ways as well.

Many Apache, however, did not like farming. Apache men

missed hunting. They preferred it to the tasks associated with planting and farming. Even if they had been willing, their land would have been difficult to farm. Whites had already taken over most of the good farmland available. What was left was too dry to grow crops.

Losing Ground

As poor as the land was, it was all the reservation Apache had. They lived in fear that the U.S. government would take their reservations away. The Jicarilla, for instance, had lived on their reservation for only a few years when the United States decided to move them again. Against their will, the Jicarilla were sent to live on the Mescalero reservation. The Jicarilla were unhappy sharing the Mescalero's land. The Jicarilla's leaders finally convinced U.S. officials to grant them a new reservation in 1887.

The Mescalero had their own problems holding on to their lands. Officials kept sending other Apache groups to their reservation without the Mescalero's permission. In 1903, thirty-seven Lipan Apache from Mexico were moved onto the Mescalero's lands. Nine years later, 171 Chiricahua Apache joined them as well. They were from the group of Chiricahua held at Fort Sill, Oklahoma. In 1913, the United States gave the Fort Sill Chiricahua the choice of staying there or moving to the Mescalero reservation. Most chose to return to the Southwest, even though they would have to live in Mescalero territory.

At first, there were tensions between the Mescalero, Chiricahua, and Lipan. They settled in different parts of the reservation and avoided each other. But over time, the three groups learned to live comfortably with one another. They eventually all merged into the modern Mescalero Apache Tribe.

Building a Future

For all reservation Apache, making a living was a challenge. The people of the Mescalero and Jicarilla reservations had some success raising sheep and cattle. In the twentieth century, they also began selling timber cut from reservation forests. The Jicarilla found additional revenue by leasing mineral-rich lands to gas and oil companies.

These businesses, though, provided few jobs. To earn a living, many Apache began working for non-Indians for wages. In order to find work, many had to move closer to the **agency**, the building where the agent lived and worked. As a result, most reservation residents came to live in or near small towns that built up around the agencies.

After decades of reservation life, the Apache were still struggling. Most reservation Apache were poor. Many suffered from poor health and were often hungry. Their housing and schools were far worse than those available to other Americans.

In the 1930s, even the U.S. Congress had to admit that Indian reservations were not being well run. In a law known as

the Indian Reorganization Act, it offered tribes the opportunity to form their own governments so they could make more decisions affecting their reservations. For many Indians, including several Apache groups, this marked a new beginning. For years, U.S. officials had told the Apache what to do. Now, they would finally have a chance to shape their own future.

The Apache living on the reservations faced many hardships. There were few job opportunities and schools. Many people had health problems and not enough food to eat.

Today, many Apache still live on reservations. The White Mountain Apache tribe lives on the Fort Apache reservation and runs several businesses, including a resort, a casino, and a cultural museum.

Chapter Six

The Apache Today

The early years of reservation life were hard for the Apache. Many still struggle today with unemployment and poverty. The Apache people have not only survived difficult times. In some ways, they have thrived. Especially in recent decades, the Apache, with the help of their tribal governments, have worked hard to improve their lives and strengthen their ties to one another. As they have prospered, their population has grown. They are now the seventh

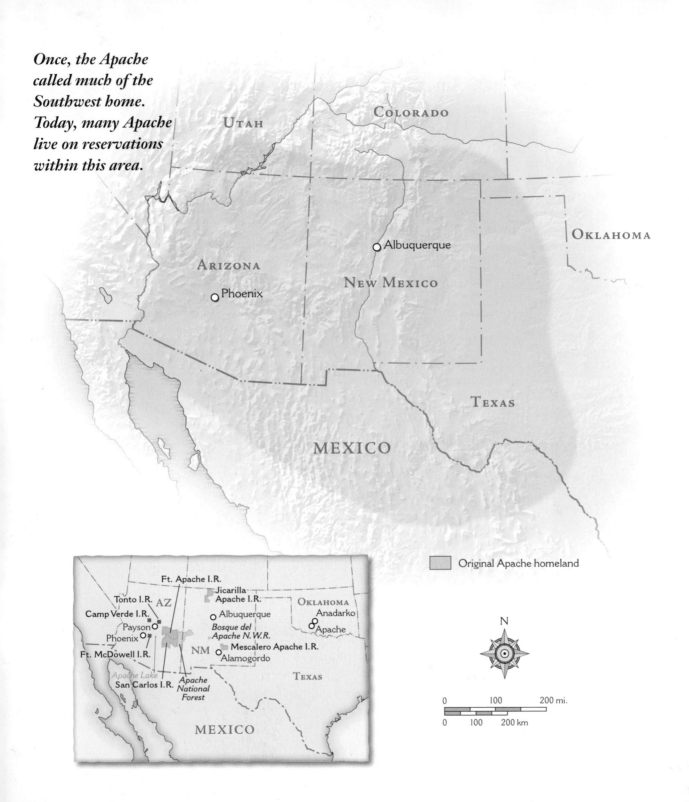

Once, the Apache called much of the Southwest home. Today, many Apache live on reservations within this area.

COLORADO

UTAH

OKLAHOMA

ARIZONA

NEW MEXICO

Albuquerque

Phoenix

TEXAS

MEXICO

Original Apache homeland

Ft. Apache I.R.

Jicarilla
Apache I.R.

Tonto I.R. AZ

OKLAHOMA

Camp Verde I.R.

Albuquerque

Anadarko

Payson

*Bosque del
Apache N.W.R.*

Apache

Phoenix

Ft. McDowell I.R.

NM

Mescalero Apache I.R.

Alamogordo

Apache Lake

TEXAS

San Carlos I.R.

Apache
National
Forest

MEXICO

N

0   100   200 mi.

0   100   200 km

46

largest Indian group in the United States. According to the 2000 census, about 97,000 Americans claim Apache ancestry.

Today, there are some Apache living in nearly every state. But the states with the biggest Apache populations are New Mexico, Arizona, and Oklahoma. Many Apache live on two reservations in New Mexico and five reservations in Arizona. There are also Apache communities in Anadarko, Oklahoma; Apache, Oklahoma; and Payson, Arizona.

Allan Houser

A descendant of the famous Chiricahua leader Mangas Coloradas, Allan Houser is considered one of the greatest American Indian artists. Born in 1914, he started his career as a painter, but later taught himself to sculpt. He is best known for his sculptures of Apache warriors, dancers, and mothers. In 1992, Houser became the first Indian to receive the National Medal of Arts. His works are now found in art museums around the world.

Welcoming Tourists

To produce income for their people and their governments, the Apache have long looked to the natural resources of their tribal lands. For many years, various Apache groups have made money from timber, gas, and oil. But increasingly they are turning to **tourism** to fund their tribes. Every year, thousands of people visit an Apache reservation while vacationing in the Southwest.

The Jicarilla Indian Reservation is a favorite spot for outdoor sports. With seven lakes and mountain views, it offers fishing, boating, camping, and hiking. For hunters, the reservation has the Horse Lake Mesa Game Park, which houses a huge herd of elk.

Eager to ski, many vacationers visit the Sunrise Park Resort in Arizona's White Mountains. This resort is operated by the Apache of the Fort Apache Indian Reservation, who now call themselves the White Mountain Apache. They also hope to refurbish the old army fort there and turn it into a tourist

The Mescalero operate a luxury resort where people can enjoy a variety of activities, including golf.

attraction. Fort Apache is famous throughout the world because it is the setting of many popular movie westerns.

Since the mid-1970s, the Mescalero Indian Reservation has been a tourist destination. There, the Mescalero operated for many years the successful Inn of the Mountain Gods, a luxury hotel. The tribe recently tore down the inn to make way for new resort, which will include a hotel, casino, spa, and four restaurants. The Mescalero also run the Ski Apache Resort and the Mescalero Travel Center. Located on an isolated stretch of highway, the center is a convenient place for travelers to stop for food and gas.

Traditions Old and New

These businesses have helped fund many improvements on Apache reservations. The residents of Mescalero enjoy a community building that includes a swimming pool, bowling alley, and meeting rooms. The tribe also runs the Mescalero Family Center, which provides housing and care for the elderly.

In 2002, the Mescalero opened a new school. Educating students from kindergarten to twelfth grade, the $37-million complex has a television studio, football stadium, five-hundred-seat auditorium, and two softball fields.

To keep knowledge of their past alive, the residents of San Carlos and Fort Apache operate cultural centers

This basket is just one example of Jicarilla crafts.

and museums. At the Jicarilla Indian Reservation, visitors can stop by the Jicarilla Arts and Crafts Shop and Museum. On display are samples of traditional Jicarilla crafts, including basketry, beadwork, and leatherwork.

The Mescalero are preserving their old ways through the Traditional Counseling Program. It brings young people together with elders, who tell them about how the Apache used to live. Although most Apache now speak English, many Apache children still learn the Apache language either at home or in classes at reservation schools.

Preserving Tradition

The Apache also treasure their religious traditions. Most reservations holds ceremonies at specific times each year. In the first week in July, the Mescalero hosts an Indian dance and rodeo. As part of the festivities, they perform the ancient Apache ceremony to celebrate the girls' passage to womanhood. Non-Indians are now invited to attend the ceremony, as long as remain quiet and respectful.

Each September, the Jicarilla hold a two-day tribal holiday and harvest celebration. As part of the event, two teams run a relay race. The race reenacts a contest between the sun and moon told of in the Apache's ancient stories. By holding this festival, the Jicarilla hope to ensure that all tribal members will have good health and plenty of food in the year to come.

An Apache dancer performs during the annual Mescalero dance and rodeo event.

In recent decades, Apache religious leaders have led a movement to protect Mount Graham. Located in Arizona near San Carlos, the mountain is sacred to the Apache. It is the home of the **Gaan**, mountain spirits that protect them against illness and danger. The University of Arizona is building telescopes on Mount Graham, which the Apache feel endangers this holy site. The Apache have attracted enormous attention to the cause, rallying the support of more than one hundred religious and environmental groups the world over. As their passionate campaign shows, the Apache spirit is alive and well. Like their ancestors, today's Apache are fighters, willing to face any struggle to preserve the Apache way.

Timeline of the Apache

About 1400	Ancestors of the Apache arrive in the American Southwest.
Mid-1500s	Spanish arrive in Apache territory.
1786	Spanish leader Bernardo de Gálvez recommends negotiating peace with Apache groups.
1821	Mexico gains control of Apache territory formerly claimed by Spain.
1848	Apache lands come under U.S. control at the end of the Mexican-American War.
1858	Chiricahua leader Cochise negotiates peace with U.S. officials at Apache Pass.
1861	U.S. army takes Cochise hostage during the "Cut the Tent" Incident. U.S. soldiers pull out of the Southwest as the American Civil War begins.
1863	The Mescalero Apache are forcibly moved to Bosque Redondo. Chiricahua leader Mangas Coloradas is murdered by U.S. troops.
1871	About one hundred Western Apache are killed by a non-Indian mob during the Camp Grant Massacre. The U.S. government establishes the San Carlos Apache Reservation in present-day Arizona.
1872	Cochise meets with General O. O. Howard in the Dragoon Mountains.
1873	The Mescalero Apache are granted a reservation in what is now New Mexico.

1880	Mexican soldiers defeat the Chiricahua Apache led by Victorio.
1886	Chiricahua leader Geronimo surrenders to U.S. authorities.
1887	The U.S. government establishes a permanent reservation for the Jicarilla in what is now New Mexico.
1903	The Lipan Apache of Mexico are sent to live on the Mescalero's reservation.
1912	The United States allows the Chiricahua held at Fort Sill, Oklahoma, to relocate to the Mescalero Indian Reservation.
1930s	Several Apache groups establish tribal governments under rules set out by the Indian Reorganization Act.
1975	The Mescalero Apache establish the Inn of the Mountain Gods.
1988	The Apache begin their battle to preserve the sacred Mount Graham in Arizona.
2000	The U.S. Census names the Apache the seventh largest Indian group in the United States.

Glossary

agency—the building where a reservation agent works and lives

agent—an employee of the U.S. government charged with overseeing an Indian reservation

Gaan—mountain spirits that the Apache believe protect them from harm

massacre—the killing of a large number of people

missionary—a person who tries to convert others to his or her religion

rations—fixed portions of food

reservation—a tract of land assigned to an Indian group for its exclusive use

scout—a person sent ahead of an army to gather information about the location and condition of the enemy

shaman—a religious leader with the special knowledge needed to perform ceremonies

tipi—a portable cone-shaped dwelling made from a frame of wooden poles covered with animal hides

tourism—the business of providing lodging and services to people vacationing in an area

treaty—a formal agreement between two nations

tribe—a group of related Indians who share the same customs and language

wickiup—a dome-shaped dwelling covered with grass, brush, or animal hides

To Find Out More

Books

Aleshire, Peter. *Reaping the Whirlwind: The Apache Wars*. New York: Facts on File, 1998.

Englar, Mary. *The Apache: Nomadic Hunters of the Southwest*. Mankota, Minn.: Bridgestone Books, 2003.

Golston, Sydele E. *Changing Woman of the Apache: Women's Lives in Past and Present*. New York: Franklin Watts, 1996.

Hoyt-Goldsmith, Diane. *Apache Rodeo*. New York: Holiday House, 1995.

Netzley, Patricia D. *Apache Warriors*. San Diego: KidHaven, 2002.

Seymour, Tryntje Van Ness. *The Gift of Changing Woman*. New York: Henry Holt, 1993.

Sneve, Virginia Driving Hawk. *The Apaches*. New York: Holiday House, 1997.

Thompson, William and Dorcas Thompson. *Geronimo*. Broomhall, Penn.: Chelsea House, 2002.

Organizations and Online Sites

Children of Changing Woman
http://www.peabody.harvard.edu/maria/Cwoman.html
This site about traditional Apache life is based on an exhibition at Harvard University's Peabody Museum curated by Ernestine Cody, herself a member of the Western Apache tribe.

Fort Apache Indian Reservation
http://www.wmat.nsn.us
This Web site focuses on the history, culture, and ways of the people of the Fort Apache Indian Reservation (also known as the White Mountain Apache Reservation) in Arizona.

Jicarilla Indian Reservation

http://www.jicarillaonline.com

The Jicarilla's Web site includes information on the tribe's history and government, as well as photographs showing the natural beauty of their New Mexico reservation.

A Note on Sources

There are many excellent books about the Apache, especially those dealing with their conflicts with the U.S. army during the nineteenth century. Two solid overviews of Apache history are Donald E. Worcester's *The Apaches: Eagles of the Southwest* (University of Oklahoma Press, 1979) and Frank C. Lockwood's *The Apache Indians* (University of Nebraska Press, 1987). Michael E. Melody's *The Apache* (Chelsea House, 1989) is also a brief but good general introduction. Helpful scholarly assessments of the major Apache groups are available in the *Handbook of North American Indians, Vol. 10* (Smithsonian Institution, 1988). Also recommended is Sherry Robinson's *Apache Voices: Their Stories of Survival as Told to Eve Ball* (University of New Mexico Press, 2000). This collection of interviews provides a fascinating look into the Apache's perspective on the Apache Wars and the subsequent reservation era.

—Liz Sonneborn

Index

Numbers in *italics* indicate illustrations.

About the Author

Liz Sonneborn is a writer and an editor, living in Brooklyn, New York. A graduate of Swarthmore College, she specializes in books about the history and culture of American Indians and the biographies of noteworthy people in American history. She has written more than forty books for children and adults, including *A to Z of Native American Women* (Facts on File, 1997) and *The New York Public Library's Amazing Native American History* (John Wiley, 1999), winner of a Parent's Choice Award.